WRITING WITH CATS

AN INSPIRATIONAL AND PRACTICAL GUIDE FOR WRITERS

By

Gerald J. Schiffhorst, Ph.D.

BUTLER HOUSE

Publications

2003

Library of Congress
Control Number: 2003096175
ISBN Number 0-9745531-0-7

To order copies of this book or find more about
the author, contact www.writingcats.com. To
send comments or questions to the author,
contact Butler House Publications, Winter Park,
Florida at this address: schiffhorst@yahoo.com

TO

Lynn, Laurie, and, of course, Lizzie

"Time spent with cats is never wasted."

--Colette

"If you want to be a published novelist..., the best thing you can do is keep a pair of cats."

--Aldous Huxley

"Authors like cats because they are such quiet, lovable, wise creatures, and cats like authors for the same reasons."

--Robertson Davies

TABLE OF CONTENTS

- Preface

- **Part I. The Muse that *Mews*:**
  The Writer and the Contemplative Cat

  A Partial Listing of Some Notable
  Authors' Cats

  Some Notable English-Language Poets
  Who Have Immortalized Their Cats

- **Part II. From Visions to Revisions:**
  A Practical Guide to Writing

  Recommended Reading

- **Part III. Your Journal:**
  Writing with Cats

PREFACE

As you will see in this book, I believe that cats should be taken seriously, as a writer's best friend and source of inspiration. Cats, being both reflective and practical, are invaluable to anyone interested in writing. I do not pretend that cats write: they have no need to. But by their very nature, they embody the essential quality that every writer needs—and every reader appreciates—especially the gifts of deep reflection and playful imagination. Their quiet inspiration is one of the great secrets of literary history, and their many practical as well as spiritual assets can no longer be ignored.

Sadly, some authors put the word *cats* in their book titles mainly to call attention to their work and increase sales. This is an unfortunate trivializing of the feline genius. When he published *Golfing for Cats* some years ago, the British satirist Alan Coren made it clear in his preface that his book had nothing whatsoever to do with either golf *or* cats but that these words were part of the title to help sell the book. Not all writers are so honest in using cats.

Some authors exploit cats by putting them to work in their stories. Some mystery writers describe feline sleuths talking on the telephone or using the computer to solve crimes, of all things! Such gimmicks might help sell books but do considerable damage to the image of cats by showing them in demeaning, unnatural roles, making them laughable.

So a serious study of the relation of cats and writers is long overdue. This book is an effort in that direction. Perhaps one day, scholars and critics interested in literary influence will address the role of cats, and experts in the writing process will consider the feline aspects of composition. Until that time comes, this modest book will have to suffice.

I do not propose to tell the full story of how cats inspire writers. Given the mystery of both cats and creativity, this would be impossible. Rather, I hope to set the record straight about the real feline influence on writers so that we might learn more from our cats and give them proper credit as authentic collaborators. I also show how would-be authors can understand more about the writing process and feel more confident about themselves by observing their cats.

So, whether you are a writer or a cat-lover-- or both--I hope this book appeals to you. If you are a writer who wants to be an author, or if you merely want to improve your writing, you will see that Part I is intended to provide inspiration as well as entertainment, helping you relax. And you will realize how many great thinkers and writers have valued cats as literary companions. As you focus on the more practical tips in Part II, I hope you will return to Part I at your leisure. And you might use the Journal section (Part III) to record your reactions to what you have read.

If you are mainly a cat-lover, you will be most interested in Part I. The second half of the book will provide a pleasant (I hope) extension of the opening essay, and you will probably find that, being a reader, you are like a cat in that you, too, enjoy the company of writers. And you might become inspired to begin writing.

Of course, you could be like me, keenly interested in <u>both</u> feline behavior and writing. As such, you are my ideal reader and will, I hope, find the whole book worthwhile. If so, you might recommend it to your friends. If you have comments and suggestions, feel free to use the e-mail address to contact me. In any case, I hope the book will motivate you to write.

Most writers I have known agonize over some aspect of the writing process. It seems that writing and worrying are often inseparable. I have helped thousands of students in more than 35 years of college teaching become better writers. I have done so in part by combining reassurances along with humor. I hope that my advice—along with the anecdotes, quotations, and illustrations—will help you worry less and write more confidently.

Like every writer, I am indebted to many friends who inspired and encouraged me to complete this book. Chief among these are those to whom the book is dedicated: Lizzie, our cat, who inspired the project and graciously posed for the photos; Lynn Butler Schiffhorst, my wife, muse, and best human friend, who provides daily doses of humor, inspiration, and encouragement; and Laurie McNear, who believed from the beginning that this project had serious merit and made invaluable editorial and design contributions. Paul McNear not only made wonderful design suggestions but also generously supported the development of the book from its inception. I am grateful to Carole McDaniel for beautifully designing the book and to E. M. Rees, Susan Hubbard, and Kelle Groom for reacting so favorably to the project. Several friends, including John McCarey and Jim Rucquoi, made valuable comments about the manuscript in its earlier stages, for which I am grateful. I am also indebted to my many students at the University of Central Florida and elsewhere, over many years, for reminding me of the rewards and challenges of teaching writing.

Gerald J. Schiffhorst
Winter Park, Florida

Part I. THE MUSE THAT *MEWS*:
The Writer and the
Contemplative Cat

Writers and cats naturally fit together. I tell my students, "if you are serious about writing, don't buy a new computer; what you need is a cat." This often takes some explaining. Many people simply assume that writers are attracted to cats because they're quiet or mysterious creatures—or both; but with cats, as with writers, nothing is simple.

Joyce Carol Oates, in *The Sophisticated Cat*, is not alone in observing that authors have often been drawn to cats, but, like so many other writers, she doesn't explore why. This is what I propose to do. And I will also show why cats are a much-overlooked source of inspiration.

I have no patience with authors who write sentimental stories about cats or who describe the amusing antics of their pets, as if the purpose of feline existence were frivolous. What goes on in the feline mind needs to be taken seriously. This includes recognizing that cats are also attracted to writers; they know kindred spirits.

If we are fortunate, our cats will help immortalize us as they have immortalized other, famous writers. Yes, writers have given fame to their cats, but the deeper truth is that cats have been the source of inspiration for more lines of unforgettable literature than we will ever know. Writers can apply the feline genius for reflection, imagination, and fussiness to their own work, from visions and planning to revisions. First, let's consider the literary attributes of cats.

If you have ever observed cats, you know that they have innate abilities that naturally lend themselves to the literary life. Dreaming is what cats do best, and as such they set a high standard for authors, especially those who worry that time spent merely reflecting is somehow wasted.

There is much more to the cat's genius than mere reverie, however. The cat has an enviably rich and unlimited inner life, most of it inaccessible to us. And this is its greatest asset to people who write.

CATS AND CONTEMPLATION

Although my experience as a writer and as a teacher of writing stretches over thirty-five years, my intimate experience with cats has been limited to several years' association with a tabby named Lizzie. Yet I understand that her behavior is sufficiently typical of the species to warrant some comments on the contemplative life of cats.

So, before outlining the literary attributes of felines, and their influence on many distinguished writers, I think it best to put cats into an even broader spiritual context: that of the hallowed meditative tradition, which I often recommend to students who experience writer's block. (See also Part II.) This meditative (or contemplative) tradition, whether it is part of religious practice or not, means concentrating the mind and freeing it from extraneous thoughts. One way to do this is to focus on a repeated word or image until you feel centered and focused. Doing this for fifteen minutes or more can help you be more open to inspiration before you write.

What we easily overlook is that cats provide us with models of meditation. Since their very way of being is purely contemplative, it is easy to assume that cats staring into space are doing nothing when, in fact, they are deep in thoughts we can never fathom. Feline companions remind writers of the importance of contemplation.

Most people, when they hear the term "contemplative life," think of monks or nuns living in a cloistered community. While not limiting ourselves to those who pursue this vocation, we might consider some of the main features of the contemplative life, as it has been lived for centuries. We will then see how easily cats can be called contemplatives since they embody the following attributes:

- Solitude. Seeking a space apart from the daily hurly-burly is essential if one is to be serious about exploring the inner life. Cats, of course, are generally solitary creatures who spend much time in private reflection and thoughtful observation.

- Stability. Many monks take vows of stability, promising to live out their lives in a single cloistered environment. Cats make their sacred space and are happiest in their familiar territory. They have no need to take vows, for they are stable by nature.

- Simplicity. Every spiritual tradition teaches the need to focus on what is essential in life. What could be simpler than a cat's diet and lifestyle?

- Patience. Waiting with hope in the face of fear or difficulty is also important to contemplative spirituality. Cats have the ability to wait without knowing they are waiting.

- Silence. See discussion below.

- Love. This needs no discussion.

In addition, there are many traditional meditative techniques, such as mindful breathing, proper posture, and other habits that we humans must work on, sometimes with exhausting concentration, to become centered in our preparation for writing. All these a cat does by its very nature, without so much as a twitch of a whisker.

Cats are incapable of being bored in their contemplative meditations. Boredom involves a fear of running out of things to do, and since domesticated cats are born to do nothing (in the usual sense), they are incapable of such fear. What might seem boring to us in their lives is the very soulful reflection that writers need to cultivate.

The inner resources of a cat are an inexhaustible source of contentment.

SILENCE AND FELINE SPIRITUALITY

When I look closely at Lizzie's ears, with their many twitching muscles, I know that her feline mind is focused and alert. She has the gift of deep listening and is attuned to the sounds of nature, with their endlessly fascinating harmonies. You may think this is merely instinctive and not spiritual at all, that she is really on the lookout for mice or lizards or smaller game.

But the ability to listen in silence to the spirit deep within for hours on end is the goal of mature meditation. I have read about monks in the desert who would have given their hair shirts for the kind of concentrated attention that Lizzie has naturally.

In their wordless world, cats know that silence is not the absence of sound; it is about presence. It is being suspended in the eternal present, outside of time; this is what the great mystics have written about. I do not claim that Lizzie is a great mystic, but she has the gift of being silently, fully in the present, and open to the presence of the spirit.

Like other felines, Lizzie has no sense of the past; she lives in a world in which there are no clocks or days or years, only the constant, timeless moment. She does not bother reviewing past problems or worrying about the future, which is as unreal and irrelevant to her as the past. This is the state of mindfulness that is the aim of Eastern and Western spiritual masters: the quality of focusing intently on the reality of the present. Writers achieve this type of self-transcendence often with great effort and then usually for only short periods. Cats, however, have this talent and seem to possess it to a more heightened degree than other animals. Rather than do anything that we humans identify as productive activity, they simply are.

Although Thomas Merton, the American monk and writer, was probably not considering cats at the time, what he said about the contemplative life surely applies to the inner peace of the feline mind: "the true journey of life is within." Lizzie and her fellow cats would agree. She has no interest in going beyond her own territory and, being an indoor cat, takes great pleasure in being cloistered; she seems especially happy in our library. How far she is able to travel in her reveries is one of life's great mysteries, but I can tell that she savors every opportunity for reflection.

"All shall be well, and all manner of thing shall be well": it takes the special trust of a cat owner to make such a statement. It was written in the 14th century by Julian of Norwich, one of the great medieval mystics and the first female author in English. It is no accident that Julian was accompanied in her solitude by a cat. Her words were quoted by T. S. Eliot, famous for his verses about cats, in his poems on time and the timeless, *Four Quartets*. Do literary critics study the influence of cats on such great poetry or include cats in their theories? Sadly, the answer is 'no.'

One might expect a book called the *Poetics of Reverie*, by Gaston Bachelard, to include references to cats, but, again, they are lacking. I have read many valuable studies about the inner life from the literary and spiritual perspectives, all of them incomplete: Where are the cats? Why have they not been credited as sources of inspiration?

The Buddhist monk Thich Nhat Hanh reminds us that meditation involves stopping, calming oneself, and looking deeply into the soul; he has written eloquently about mindfulness--being totally aware of immediate reality. What he overlooks is that cats can be the best reminders we have of the power of the present moment. Whether Lizzie is licking her paws or walking gingerly toward her food bowl, she expresses the peace of being totally absorbed in the reality of the now.

This is also true when she plays. What is a clearer indication of spiritual vitality than the ability to delight in play? Who can spend time with a cat and not be amused? "Joy is the most infallible sign of the presence of God," Léon Bloy wrote. Again, I find no authors who connect this truth with cats. Since the work of writing takes serious effort and concentration; the inspired playfulness of the cat is often just what is needed to relieve a writer's tension. Although Lizzie, like all cats, may look serious and unsmiling, we know that her life is a series of simple, happy pleasures. Unfamiliar with work, she is a welcome reminder that there is a world of pure existence more important than our immediate tasks.

There is a widespread bias against feline inspiration among many literary experts, as in this statement by the poet and critic Stephen Spender: "The inner life is regarded by most *people* as so dangerous that it cannot be revealed openly and directly." Notice that telling word people. Cats do not presume to express their reflections in print and would laugh their secret cat-laugh at Spender's remark.

Cats are attuned to the dangers that threaten their external world. But they are blessed by being absolutely immune to any fear of the inner world—and it is that inner world that writers and poets strive to articulate. Authors who have the good sense to keep cats near at hand would seem, then, to have major advantages.

One contemporary author who makes admirable use of his feline companion is James P. Carse. In his essay, "A Philosopher Needs a Cat," he muses about his cat Charlie's lack of speech: "I can see that Charlie is silent, but what he is silent about, what he would say if that silence broke, I don't even know how to imagine."

Carse goes on to say that, when we look at another person, especially someone intentionally silent, we expect a spoken response:

We expect the disciplined silence of a master to issue in speech, and the deeper the silence the deeper the speech that rises from it. From the Buddha, whose face is the very image of desirelessness, empty of both comprehension and incomprehension, has come an ever-expanding ocean of written and spoken wisdom. . . . Although Charlie's face has the same absence of both comprehension and incomprehension as the Buddha's, it does not suggest an ocean of words needing to be spoken. The animal's face warns us that we might have it backwards. Instead of the speech that comes after silence, we begin to wonder at the possibility of a silence that comes both before and after speech. (20)

This author is interested in the soul and in what he calls "the mysticism of ordinary experience." Not surprisingly, his cat has inspired some original insights on silence.

All writers can benefit, I think, from wordless meditation as a way to prepare for writing. Many also benefit by relaxing with simple stretching exercises and deep breathing. Whatever method you choose, it is obvious from what we have seen so far that cats can provide daily guidance to writers in these basic techniques.

CATS AND THE WRITING PROCESS

What else do cats offer writers that make them a source of inspiration and, even, ideal collaborators? As I tell my students, the most challenging aspect of the writing process, and the one most difficult to teach, is thinking—not only of what to write about but how to develop it. (See Part II.)   Developing a topic leads to the need for specificity.

Begin, I tell them, with close observation of the natural world, then describe what you see. Notice how cats, with exquisite sensitivity, observe every detail around them, then take all the time they need to play with and think through their options, whether to pounce or wait or conserve their energy. Writers, too often, overconfidently rush to the first topic that comes to mind, fearing that the time tossing ideas around is somehow wasted. They might thereby bypass a significant idea that is worth developing.

Cats are much more keen in their observations than many of my students, and they are very specific in their tastes. Cats have a discriminating refinement in this area. Lizzie, for example, will select one small area of our garden to focus on for hours, and she will take in every detail of this area. This is the wisdom of the cat: to know that truth lies hidden in the details of everyday life.

Here is a short list of essential attributes that writers must have or cultivate, all of which cats possess in abundance:

- Introspection
- Intelligence
- Skill in observation
- Emotional openness
- Curiosity
- Patience
- Imagination
- Sensitivity

There can be no doubt that cats are intelligent—but too smart to let on that they are; and too sharp to be exploited or harnessed to a task.

Several experts have recently attested to the non-human capacity for intellectual activity. In his 2003 book, *Thinking Without Words*, José Luis Bermudes argues that animals are genuine thinkers. Penelope Smith in *When Animals Speak* discusses the way people learn spiritual lessons from non-human creation. And, speaking of cats, the scientist William Jordan, author of *A Cat Named Darwin*, says, "You do not communicate with a cat. You commune. Your inner lizard and his inner lizard connect. Not with words or thoughts, but with gestures, postures, sounds that are basically emotional."

Roger Caras, who has written widely about animals, has a book, *A Cat Is Watching*, that shows how and why cats enjoy watching people, perhaps, he suggests, because they understand us in ways we cannot fathom. A cat enjoys contemplating and evaluating us "as part of its long-range store of information about the human race" (150). How cats think may be a mystery, but that they do so is widely accepted by scientists. Calling cats cognitive creatures,

Caras says that, if you combine feline conditioning, genetic programming, excellent senses, and keen powers of observation with a unique type of concentration, you have an exceptionally bright and sensitive creature that has managed to survive difficult times for at least four millennia.

Emotional intelligence has rightly been applied to cats. Emily Brontë, author of *Wuthering Heights*, not only confessed her affection for cats but stated, "A cat is an animal which has more human feeling than almost any other." Since all great authors speak to the heart, it is no wonder that so many of them find in the cat a kindred spirit with a hidden reservoir of feelings we can only guess at. Caras says that, in their various calls and cries, cats register not only various types of anger but warning, pain, surprise, pleading, excitement, concern, complaint as well as sexual invitation and satisfaction.

We should never underestimate what a cat knows. By "knowledge" I don't mean facts but thoughts and the emotional communing with us that cat-owners enjoy. Since many philosophers tell us that thinking is ultimately wordless, cats do not need human language to think. I also include, as part of intelligence, intuition, which my dictionary defines as "the direct perception of truths," immediate apprehension, and keen and quick insight. Doesn't this definition apply to cats? Ideas and intuitive emotion "recollected in tranquility" (in Wordsworth's phrase) are what the serious author begins with. Is it any wonder that observing cats can help you excel as a writer?

La Fontaine in the 17th century was one of the first of a long line of distinguished French writers to praise the feline mind. He said that the intelligence of cats is greater than that of dogs and uncomfortably close to that of human beings. Another Frenchman, Théophile Gautier (d. 1872), wrote that "the cat is a philosopher, sedate, tranquil, a creature of habit, a lover of decency and order." (The same author stated, "Only a Frenchman could understand the fine and subtle qualities of the cat.") And the philosopher Hippolyte Taine (d. 1893) went so far as to say that "I have studied many philosophers and many cats. The wisdom of cats is infinitely superior." We all know how serious and rational the French are supposed to be, so it is all the more significant that dozens of French writers, from Montaigne to Colette, have praised the cat. They would agree with the words of Sir Walter Scott (even though he was not French): "there is more passing in their [cats'] minds than we are aware of."

Jeffrey Moussaieff Masson, having studied cats with a psychologist's eye, would concur. In his 2002 book, *The Nine Emotional Lives of Cats*, he says that "cats are so curious that they are even curious about events they imagine (or remember) in their own mind."

It is easy to assume that, because cats do not speak, they are what some of our less

enlightened ancestors called "dumb beasts."
But intelligence does not have to be expressed
verbally. The famous curiosity of cats and their
sense of humor are clear signs that they are
smart. Notice how cats examine us up and
down, especially when leaving or entering their
territory, as if to find out what we are thinking.
It's as if they have what Caras calls a sixth
sense, an unknown "avenue into the reality of
their space and time" (29). Experts like Caras,
who know infinitely more about animal behavior
than I ever will, continually remind us how little
we really understand about the feline mind.

Do cats laugh? Perhaps. When Lizzie hears
me calling her and I find her hiding under the
dining room table, safely shielded by a table
cloth, she seems quite delighted to have tricked
me. Her yawn-like gesture of contentment is, for
me, like a laugh. Cats clearly enjoy making a
game of their relationship with us, especially
when we are making fools of ourselves, Caras
says, looking for them. What are humor and
trickery but signs of intelligence?

No wonder the Irish have an ancient proverb: "Never ask a cat a question; she might answer back."

Along with cats' intelligence and the gift of intuition come sensitivity and an openness to many moods. Consider the variety of feline facial expressions, unequalled (experts tell us) by any other non-human animal. They convey amusement as well as fear, triumph, playfulness as well as the other emotions Caras mentions.

Cats, moreover, are careful and notoriously neat—in marked contrast to the messy work habits of many writers. And, although cats sometimes seem too curious for their own good, curiosity, too, is essential for any writer. What does curiosity literally mean? Full of care, concern, and attention. So the famous feline virtue of curiosity is not necessarily a sign of playfulness but of caring enough to give full attention to the subject at hand, an admirable goal for any writer.

Cats, as we have seen, are also patient, waiting for hours for their prey; and writers fortunate enough to spend hours quietly in the pensive company of their cats can learn to overcome the frustration that so often comes when the words don't.

Anyone who has watched cats stalk an invisible mouse knows that they are blessed with the writer's most cherished gift: imagination. It was none other than Einstein who asserted, "imagination is more significant than knowledge." There is no reason to limit this observation to the human species. Lizzie provides daily demonstrations of her vivid imagination: she treats one of my old shoelaces as if it were a mouse's tail, a lizard, or perhaps a snake. She is convinced that behind two pillows on the sofa where she plays there lurks a tiny creature, probably with a tail, that will emerge if she waits long enough. She also imagines my hand as a paw to be swatted, batted, and, if possible, bitten. Lynn and I must appear to her either as moving furniture to be rubbed against or as giant cats.

I agree with the novelist Aldous Huxley: "If you want to be a psychological novelist and write about human beings, the best thing you can do is keep a pair of cats." Even one might suffice. Although cats, like writers, are too individualized to be stereotyped, they possess a serious concentration that many of my student writers would do well to emulate. No book or software program on writing can provide such interior lessons.

THE MUSE THAT *MEWS*

Not surprisingly, most of the major writers who have celebrated their cats have been men. Just as poets of old were inspired by the female Muse, so more modern authors are drawn to a feminine source of inspiration, which often takes feline form. There is no need to rehearse the many feminine attributes of the cat. But it is helpful to acknowledge the connection between cats and the Muses of classical mythology, daughters of Jupiter and Memory. That there were traditionally nine of these patronesses of literature and the arts is no doubt coincidental with the legend that a cat has nine lives; what is surely not a coincidence is, first, that the word muse means "reminder" (and we know how effective the cat is as a reminder to us of the inner life); second, that cats possess exemplary memories, another literary attribute; and third, that the universal sound that the cat makes—its *mews*—is identical to its ancient Greek name.

I discovered the link between muse and mews when I realized that Lizzie hardly ever says *meow*; with sensible economy, she finds one syllable sufficient to indicate that she is ready for me to give her full attention.

The femininity of the cat and her soft, sensuous appeal fascinated even Ernest Hemingway, known as much for his masculine bravado as for his writing. Like all great writers, he needed a muse that mews.

Hemingway had many cats and wrote about them. While living in Paris, he and his wife, rather than hire a baby sitter, even allowed a sensible, affectionate feline named F. Puss to watch over their infant son. This cat performed his duties admirably and with serious attention, which is more than can be said about the baby's parents.

The writer made a strong argument for the author-cat relationship when he said, "A cat has absolute emotional honesty: human beings, for one reason or another, may hide their feelings, but cats do not." Boise, his best feline friend in Cuba, appears in *Islands in the Stream*. Although this is a big, black tomcat who sires a cat named Goat ("a big-shouldered, heavy-necked, wide-faced, tremendous-whiskered, black, fighting cat"), it is clear that the real appeal of cats to Hemingway was their emotional openness and essential femininity. He certainly enjoyed their sensitivity and unpredictability. And he would be pleased that some sixty felines, including descendants of a polydactyl (six-toed) cat from the 1930s, grace his Key West home today. Appropriately, some bear such names as James Joyce and Emily Dickinson.

"Papa" Hemingway would probably not admit that many men often fear the strange inner wisdom of the cat; maybe they also have some fear of the human female for various, complicated reasons. Nor would he want to be associated with much of the sentimental or metaphysical writing about cats, even by "real men." What, for example, would he think of Jules Verne's comment that cats are "spirits come to earth"? Or with Jean Cocteau's statement, "I love cats because I enjoy my home, and little by little, they become its visible soul"?

American writers tend to be much more down to earth in their appreciation of cats. There is nothing wimpy about Mark Twain's writing about cats, which is also extensive. He kept eleven cats on his Connecticut farm. "If man could be crossed with the cat, it would improve man, but it would deteriorate the cat," he wrote.

He also said that, "if animals could speak, the dog would be a blundering, outspoken fellow, but the cat would have the rare grace of never saying a word too much."

The silence and mystery of the cat are a recurring source of fascination to writers. The great Russian writer Anton Chekhov, who included cats in several of his stories, wrote that "the soul of another is a mystery, and a cat's soul is even more so." This brings us back to the link between feline spirituality and literary inspiration. Cats have a sense of the depth of life's mysteries. Roger Caras, who steers clear of most mystical interpretations of feline behavior, wonders if the faraway look in cats' eyes means that they are "listening to an inner music, an inner truth." (139). I don't think there is much doubt about the mysterious wisdom of the feline soul. As another expert on cats has written, "Perhaps cats, as visionaries, know that one day speech itself will pass from human consciousness and we will live in telepathic bliss. . . .Do cats, having done away with

language as we know it, await the day?"
(Hausman, *The Mythology of Cats*) As one
writer, Nan Porter, remarked, "If cats could talk,
they wouldn't."

But, of course, they do talk, making a wide
range of sounds that clearly constitute a
language. While Lizzie often shrieks at intruding
cats, on at least one occasion we heard her
singing, in a beautiful, magical communion with
another feline soul; for about five minutes, their
harmony rose and fell like waves. They did not
need our type of speech.

They seem to enjoy listening to our speech,
and many writers have both talked and listened
to their cats. Raymond Chandler, famous for his
tough-guy detective stories, talked to his black
Persian, Taki, as though she were human; he
called her his secretary because she sat on his
manuscripts as he tried to revise them. Damon
Runyon, no softie either, cherished his cat
Lillian and wrote about her.

At the end of this chapter, I list many of the famous authors and their equally famous felines. I have also listed some of the notable poets who have immortalized cats.

THE ROLE OF CATS IN LITERARY HISTORY

There is enough material on writers and their cats to fill an entire volume. Here are a few irresistible anecdotes that will help convince you that, if you want to be a serious writer, a cat might be your best friend.

One of the most famous literary cats was Hodge, the pet of Samuel Johnson. The great 18th century man of letters would trust none of the servants to buy oysters for the cat, so Dr. Johnson himself visited the fishmonger daily. Who opened those oysters and placed them on the floor for Hodge? None other than Dr. Johnson himself. Boswell, Johnson's biographer, gives us the delicious details of Dr. Johnson's affection for Hodge. But, typically, nothing is said about the influence of Hodge on

Johnson's extensive literary output: would there have been all the poetry, criticism, or the 1755 dictionary (the first of its kind in English) without the calming inspiration of Hodge? It is doubtful. No writer would interrupt his work to buy oysters for his cat if he did not feel a deep sense of gratitude for the animal's inspiration. Unlike dogs, cats may not make heroic rescues, but their quiet influence on writers is un-deniable. It simply does not get recorded.

Dogs tend to get more attention in the biographies of writers than cats, and details about writers' cats, especially in earlier times, are rare. Often they are in the realm of legend, as with the feline pictured with St. Jerome as he translated the Bible, or with the Italian writer Petrarch, who popularized the sonnet; his unnamed cat was put to death and mummified upon the poet's death in 1374. Scholars tell us that his poetic muse was one Laura, but who knows for sure if this muse was human or feline?

Many wonder whether Shakespeare had a cat, although his busy life in the theatre might argue against it. We know that he disliked dogs—witness the many nasty images of curs in his plays—but did he favor cats? Since cats know the true meaning of life and since millions of readers have turned to Shakespeare to understand themselves, and life, it seems plausible that the Bard had at least one cat. (We know that his patron, the Earl of Southampton, did; she accompanied him to the Tower of London and is included in a stained glass portrait of the earl.) It is hard to imagine the writer of the sonnets unaccompanied by a reflective feline friend.

Yet the evidence of the plays is not encouraging; his characters, admittedly, say some pejorative things about felines, including many stereotyped statements intended to entertain his audience. These references are more reflective of the culture in which the plays were produced, I suggest, than of the poet's own more refined sensibility. As with religion,

Shakespeare had to be careful about revealing his true feelings. After all, this was the period when King James I (1603-25) was not only a witch hunter but thought it sporting to use cats for target practice. I am glad to say that among the short list of history's famous cat haters, there are no writers of any significance.

You might be thinking that a cat in Shakespeare's time might simply be a necessity to reduce the population of mice. Yet anyone studying what writers say about their cats would find that <u>work</u> of any kind is hardly expected. This is comforting since cats really detest work, yet whatever they do—sleeping, eating, playing— seems to be done in a state of heightened consciousness: the cat is always, to some extent, awake to the sounds of the universe. Hence its value to writers.

The life of many poets, like that of all cats, is counter-cultural in terms of the modern world. America and its imitators uphold a myth devoted to progress, productivity, and efficiency, based on the assumption that endless technological improvements will produce greater happiness. Cats, who know that happiness is to be found within, symbolize the antithesis of this philosophy: hence their appeal to serious writers. If these writers often fail to acknowledge an indebtedness to their cats, it doesn't follow that the influence of the cats has been negligible relative to their literary output, since the feline influence is something felt rather than clearly defined. Cats, who live in the realm of playful possibility, help establish a mood of reflection essential to the creation of literature.

The French poet Stephane Mallarmé (d. 1898) wrote, "mon chat est un compagne mystique." (My cat is a mystical companion.) He was writing principally about Neige (or "Snow"), the cat with whom he spent whole days alone. The poet's use of the word 'mystical' speaks volumes about the paradoxical relationship of writer and cat: those who are immersed in a world of words need the companionship and inspiration of silent creatures whose very existence suggests the reality of the eternal.

The word *inspiration* itself is revealing in our consideration of cats and literary influence. The word means, among other things, to stimulate or influence; to arouse or produce a feeling or thought; to cause, guide or motivate, as by divine or supernatural influence. Theologians have long referred to the Bible as being divinely inspired, but surely many other books have been inspired too--often, as we have seen, by that mysterious feline muse.

The notion that a cat who is not working (mousing, presumably) is no longer useful is abhorrent; it misses the whole point of feline existence--musing, which can seem pointless except to those who consider life unimaginable without great poetry, fiction, and drama. After all, great writers are guided by the heart and so know that the usefulness of the cat is beyond both reason and utility: "time spent with cats is never wasted," as Colette wrote. She was one of the few authors to give credit to her cats for some of her own qualities, including an aversion to loud noises and a need for silence. If only more writers would follow her lead.

SOME FAMOUS HISTORICAL CATS

Colette was one of many French writers indebted to cats; the others include Zola, (author of a famous story, "The Cat's Paradise"), Montaigne, Baudelaire, Rousseau, de Maupassant, Ronsard (who disliked cats but wrote about them superbly), Verlaine, Valéry, Balzac, Cocteau, Malraux, Mallarmé, Victor Hugo, and the veterinarian and cat historian Fernand Méry, who said: "With the qualities of cleanliness, discretion, affection, patience, dignity, and courage that cats have, how many of us, I ask you, would be capable of being cats?"

I should also include the writer and diplomat Francois René de Chateaubriand, who inherited a cat born in the Vatican, of all places. His name was Micetto, a gray and red cat banded with black who became the pet of Pope Leo XII in the early 19th century. Since this intellectual pope was a patron of letters and music, we can include him here, especially since he allowed Micetto to rest on his white robe as he wrote. A later pope, Pius IX, insisted that his cat enter the dining room after the soup course was served. This nameless feline used to spring onto a chair so she could sit facing the Pontiff, silently and respectfully, of course, until the meal was completed, when she would then be fed by the pope himself. Since Pius IX wrote many encyclicals, including a famous one on infallibility, is it too much to wonder if his cat influenced papal thinking? Lizzie, like all cats before her, certainly can assume an infallible, if not regal, air.

The same question of influence could be asked of Pope Gregory I, a voluminous writer known today mainly for promoting "Gregorian chant" in the late 6th century; sources indicate that this pope possessed no worldly goods except a cat, which he liked to stroke and hold in his arms while meditating. No wonder he is called Gregory the Great.

We have no evidence of these Vatican cats being baptized, but certainly they can be considered "Cat-lics." There are also famous cat-lovers in other religious traditions; Mohammad once cut off the sleeve of his robe to avoid waking a sleeping cat. (A similar story is told of the poet William Butler Yeats, who cut off part of his coat to allow a cat to sleep at the Abbey Theatre in Dublin.)

So, if history is any indication, cats have played a more significant inspirational role than most people recognize. If you're still not convinced that having a cat would improve your writing, read on.

THE REAL INFLUENCE OF CATS

You might wonder if Lizzie inspires my wife, Lynn, and me to write: isn't the answer obvious?

As Albert Schweitzer said, "there are two means of refuge from life: music and cats." We love both and agree with this statement by the Victorian writer Erasmus Darwin: "to respect the cat is the beginning of the aesthetic sense." No less an authority than Leonardo da Vinci, often called the greatest genius of the Renaissance, declared, "the smallest feline is a masterpiece." What provokes such intense admiration on the part of so many great creative minds? This book is an effort to answer that question.

In our effort to turn our lives into works of art, the cat is a model worth observing. The time and exquisite care that Lizzie takes with what might seem the most trivial detail, at least from our limited perspective, sets a very high standard. She approaches a decision about whether or not to venture onto the porch with admirable deliberation. Scratching her ear gives her more time to think as she weighs each option thoroughly. Once settled, she will spend hours in what seems like vacant staring but what is in fact what writing teachers call invention: "brainstorming" is too crude a term for the delicacy of such exploratory thinking.

After considerable rest, Lizzie is ready for limited exercise and as such mirrors our largely sedentary lives, to which she contributes more than she realizes. I am convinced that Lizzie has enhanced our writerly tendency to be nocturnal, since we tend to do our best work after sunset.

People might also wonder whether cats inspire certain types of writing. Given the feline proclivity for hunting, it might seem that the detective and mystery genres would be most influenced by cats. Edgar Allen Poe, after all, is not just famous for ravens; his chilling tale, "The Black Cat" concerns one 'Pluto,' killed, alas, by the alcoholic narrator.

Another logical feline genre would seem to be autobiography. After all, the African-American poet Countee Cullen had a cat who "wrote" an autobiography, *My Lives and How I Lost Them.*

And there have been many books of humor in the first person penned, presumably, by cats.

But it seems that, whatever specific ideas may be attributed to feline influence, our indebtedness to cats is more general; they provide writers with what they most need: a peaceful, reflective mood. They are, more than has been recognized, a genius loci or spirit of the place, establishing the atmosphere for creativity. When P. G. Wodehouse's character Lancelot Mulliner describes his cat, Webster, he pays tribute to the soul in all cats when he says that Webster gives "the impression of being a cat of deep reserves." This suggests the wellspring of imagination from which countless authors have drunk, often unaware of their feline source.

As Mildred Kirk points out in her book, *The Everlasting Cat*, writers as different as the Irish poet W. B. Yeats and the American novelist Malcolm Lowry have said that the cat was valuable as a silent witness to the scenes they created. But surely witness is not strong enough: Why are some writers reluctant to attribute influence where it is due?

Such is the legacy of the patriarchal and anthropocentric culture in which our literature has been produced: it takes for granted—or ignores--the role of the feminine, in which the cat must be included. Colette was certainly aware of this when she wrote, "there are no ordinary cats."

Charles Dickens, although he professed to preferring canines, would have agreed, especially after a special cat named Williamina came into his life. This white cat insisted on rearing her kittens in Dickens' study, despite numerous family protests, because she was especially devoted to the author. According to his daughter, Mamie, one of these kittens, called simply "the Master's Cat," stayed on for some years, following the novelist around like a dog and sitting with him while he wrote. This cat, who was deaf, had a clever way of getting attention: with her paw she would repeatedly put out the candle Dickens was reading by until she received the petting she craved. What Mamie Dickens, typically, fails to record is the scope of this cat's influence on the novels: perhaps the Master's Cat, with feline playfulness, inspired some of Dickens' great comic names or scenes. Alas, as with so many literary cats, we will never know, but perhaps this is the way cats, with their mysterious inner lives, prefer it-- to be, in Shelley's phrase, "the unacknowledged legislators of the [literary] world."

To ordinary people the cat may seem domesticated, but to poets it is symbolic of something strangely "other," its mysteries firing the imagination. Many find in cats' eyes a source of inspiration. Charles Baudelaire (d.. 1867), who would stop and pet any cat he saw in the street and who liked to have a cat in his room while writing, saw the sensuous cat as an enigmatic symbol, both soothing and disturbing, but the Symbolist poet went to extremes, sometimes imagining in the cat seemingly sinister qualities, suggesting that what attracts us to the feline personality can also present a source of mystery since it is beyond human understanding.

MORE FAMOUS FELINE COLLABORATORS

If you doubt my argument that cats are ideal literary collaborators, consider the following:

Winston Churchill, a Nobel Prize-winning author as well as statesman, had numerous cats, some serving as footwarmers. No. 10 Downing St. was ruled for a while by a black and white cat named Bob. Then Nelson, a black tabby, occupied the Cabinet Room, where he had his own chair next to the Prime Minister's as well as a place of honor at the dinner table. Churchill reportedly added a bit of brandy to his saucer of milk, a questionable but well-intentioned tribute to feline influence.

Teddy Roosevelt was famous for his cat Slippers, who would stretch out in front of the

White House State Dining Room, requiring distinguished guests to step over him. There is no record of the influence Slippers might have had on the books, speeches or other writings of "T.R."

Cats have inspired too many modern authors to list: they include J. R. R.Tolkien, Rudyard Kipling, Saki, Doris Lessing, Cleveland Amory, Sylvia Townsend Warner, and Paul Gallico, not to mention most of the pantheon of major poets in the 20th century: Ted Hughes, Elizabeth Bishop, Marianne Moore, William Carlos Williams, Randall Jarrell, Edith Sitwell, Galway Kinnell, and many others included in *The Sophisticated Cat* and other anthologies. Of course, there is also T. S. Eliot, whose book of cat poems (*Old Possum's Book of Practical Cats*) led to the Andrew Lloyd Webber musical *Cats*. Charles Elliott, who has edited *The Greatest Cat Stories Ever Told*, includes even more cat-loving writers: Beatrix Potter (who created Tom Kitten), Dorothy L. Sayers, Noel Coward, Ursula K. LeGuin, Italo Calvino, Robertson Davies, Jean

Stafford, Anne Morrow Lindbergh, Roy Blount, Jr., and the Japanese writers J. Tanizaki and S. Natsume. There are few authors in any culture, it seems, who are not attracted to cats.

An almost forgotten American poet, John Greenleaf Whittier, wrote a charming "Elegy" for his cat:

Bathsheba: to whom
None ever said scat.
No worthier cat
Ever sat on a mat
Or caught a rat:
Requies-cat.

The 18th century poet Christopher Smart is famous for having praised his cat Jeoffrey in a long, detailed poem, part of which is worth quoting:

FOR JEOFFREY   from *Jubilate Agno* (c. 1763)
For I will consider my cat Jeoffrey.
For he is the servant of the living God, duly and daily serving him.

For at the first glance at the glory of God in the
East he worships in his way.

For this is done by wreathing his body seven
times round with elegant quickness.

For when he leaps us to catch the musk, which
is the blessing of God upon his prayer.. .

For having done duty and received blessing he
begins to consider himself.

For this he performs in ten degrees.

For first he looks upon his forepaws to see if
they are clean.

For secondly he kicks up behind to clear away
there.

For thirdly he works it upon stretch with the
forepaws extended.

For fourthly he sharpens his paws by wood.

For fifthly he washes himself. . . .

For eighthly he rubs himself against a post. . . .

For tenthly he goes in quest of food.

For having considered God and himself he will
consider his neighbor.

For if he meets another cat he will kiss her in
kindness.

For when he takes his prey he plays with it to give it chance.

For one mouse in seven escapes by his dallying.

For when his day's work is done his business more properly begins.

For he keeps the Lord's watch in the night against the adversary.

For he counteracts the powers of darkness by his electrical skin and glaring eyes.

For he counteracts the devil, who is death, by brisking about the light.

For in his morning orisons he loves the sun and the sun loves him.

For he is of the tribe of tiger.

For the Cherub Cat is a term of the Angel Tiger.

For he has the subtlety and hissing of a serpent, which in goodness he suppresses...

For he purrs in thankfulness when God tells him he's a good Cat.

For he is an instrument for the children to learn benevolence upon.

For every house is incomplete without him and a blessing in lacking in spirit...

For God has blessed him in the variety of his movements.

Smart's poem, a prayer celebrating one of God's most remarkable creatures, is deservedly renowned for its attention to every detail of the cat's many attributes. Few people may read the poetry of Smart today, but many know about Jeoffrey. Smart's contemporary, Thomas Gray, wrote about his pensive Selima in the famous "Ode on the death of a favorite cat, drowned in a tub of goldfish." In that age of rationalism, the cat, after centuries of being mistreated or taken for granted, became an individual with a name and an identity, valued as a companion--not merely a household necessity associated with sinister things.

In our own era, Thomas Merton wrote extensively, as we have seen, about mystics and contemplatives, though without the aid of a cat. (Pets have not been permitted in Western monasteries in modern times; whereas in the Middle Ages, cats were the only animals allowed in the cloister, at least in England in the 13ᵗʰ century: so much for progress.)   Merton defines contemplation as the direct intuition of reality; he says it is a gift but that it involves the discipline of meditation. Cats inherit a tradition of meditation 5000 years old and certainly embody the notion of a direct intuition of reality. That is why writing and cats go together so naturally—and why Zen monasteries often have cats. Merton also remarks that the great rule about mysticism is that there are no rules: cats embody this beautifully.

"All is movement, all is rest," says the *Egyptian Book of the Dead*, written at a time when cats were worshipped as divine. What better definition of the harmonious perfection of the cat? Its tail expresses emotion; its repose expresses thoughtful reflection. All of the attributes writers need, apparently, are embodied in the cat.

When I visited New York City in 2003, I found that cats are an integral part of two literary landmarks there: At the legendary Algonquin

Hotel, home of the Round Table and birthplace of *The New Yorker*, I was not surprised to find presiding over the lobby an elegant cat named Mathilda, one of a long line of felines. Not far away, at the Gotham Book Mart, I nearly stumbled over a cat who was quite at home among the many volumes.

WHY WRITERS NEED CATS

If cats have so many literary qualities, one might be tempted to ask, why don't they actually write? For the same reason they don't talk. They don't need to: they exist on a higher plane, beyond ordinary language. You might have other reservations about my argument that cats are literary history's best-kept secret. It might be thought that their tendency to devote extensive time to sleep would limit their effectiveness as collaborators. Yet who can fault them for sleeping? Who wouldn't need rest after so many hours of intense concentration, after so many sudden bursts of energy and illumination?

To those literal-minded folk who insist that cats are merely animals, I would remind them that the word *animal* comes from the Latin *anima*, meaning breath, spirit, and soul—the very things we have explored in this part of the book.

Let us, then, honor our cats for their sensitivity and spirituality and consider them true collaborators, or at least muses, in influencing the great ideas produced by writers. Let us acknowledge in the prefaces of our books that the time spent with our cats has allowed us to absorb their finest qualities—of reflection and reverie, sensitivity and soulfulness.

Consider this comment by the authors of *Why Cats Paint*, another study of feline creativity: "The fact that cats spend more time in our company than with their own species suggests that there is something in their nature which echoes the higher levels of the human psyche" (emphasis added).

If you are a writer or student who aspires to be published yet who has lingering doubts about whether to acquire a cat, I would remind you that cats are naturally attracted to thinkers and creative people. I would urge you to look to the feline presence as a model of the contemplative, creative imagination. We writers need illumination, and the cat--a quiet reminder of the wordless mystery of a presence larger and deeper than ourselves--graciously provides it. At the very least, cats help us to smile and relax; they help us to put our lives in perspective, for we see in them the limits of being task-oriented.

In the rest of this book, I will apply these principles to some of the basic concerns many people have about the writing process.

For further information on the importance of cats in the history of literature, see Dorothy M. Stuart, *A Book of Cats* (London: Methuen, 1959). Also of value in my research have been Elizabeth Hamilton's *Cats: A Celebration* (New York: Scribner's, 1979); Roger A. Caras's *A Cat is Watching: A Look at the Way Cats See Us* (New

York: Simon and Schuster, 1989); Gerald and Loretta Hausman's *The Mythology of Cats*; Mildred Kirk, *The Everlasting Cat*; *Why Cats Paint* by Heather Busch and Burton Silver (Berkeley: Ten Speed, 1994); and J. C. Suares, *The Literary Cat*. Jean Burden's wonderful collection, *A Celebration of Cats* (New York: Eriksson, 1974) is the source of the poets on the following pages.

A Partial Listing of Some Notable Authors' Cats

Matthew Arnold: Atossa
Jeremy Bentham: Rev. Sir John Langbourne
Raymond Chandler: Taki
Collette: La Chatte (The Cat)
Winston Churchill: Nelson
Charles Dickens: Williamina (and her kitten, "the Master's Cat")
Dumas (fils), Alexandre: Mysouff
Theophile Gautier: Don Pierrot de Navarre
Thomas Gray: Selima
Ernest Hemingway: F. Puss; Boise
Victor Hugo: Chanoine
Samuel Johnson: Hodge
Jack Kerouac: Tyke
Edward Lear: Foss
D. H. Lawrence: Puss Puss
Stephane Mallarme: Neige
Mohammed: Muezza
George Moore: Jim
Edgar Allen Poe: Caterina
Theodore Roosevelt: Slippers
Damon Runyon: Lillian
Saki (H. H. Munro): Tobermory
Christopher Smart: Jeoffrey
William Makepeace Thackeray: Louisa
Mark Twain: Apollinaris, Blatherskite, Sour Mash, Tammany, Zoroaster
H. G. Wells: Mr. Peter Wells

For more such literary lore, see Carl Van Vechten, "Literary Men Who Have Loved Cats," in his 1922 book *The Tiger in the House.*

Some Notable English-Language Poets
Who Have Immortalized Cats

Poems by these and many other poets are included in *A Celebration of Cats,* edited by Jean Burden (Middlebury, Vt: Paul S. Eriksson, 1974).

American

Archibald MacLeish
Randall Jarrell
May Sarton
Marianne Moore
Philip Dacey
Wallace Stevens
Richard Eberhart
Vachel Lindsay

William Carlos Williams
Mark Van Doren
Phyllis McGinley
Denise Levertov
May Swenson
John Ciardi
Ogden Nash

British

William Cowper
Percy Bysshe Shelley
T. S. Eliot
Robert Graves
John Keats
Thomas Hardy
Christopher Smart

Thomas Gray
Edward Lear
Walter de la Mare
J. R. R. Tolkien
William Wordsworth
A. C. Swinburne

Think about what you are going to say before you write.

Photo by:
Gerald J. Schiffhorst

Time spent reflecting is never wasted.

Photo by:
Gerald J. Schiffhorst

Write about what you know. Even so, some research is often helpful.

Photo by: Gerald J. Schiffhorst

Licking prose into shape takes patience.

Photo by:
Gerald J. Schiffhorst

Read your favorite authors and soak up
their style.

Photo by:
Gerald J. Schiffhorst

Sudden insights can come at
unexpected moments.

Photo by:
Gerald J. Schiffhorst

There is a time for resting and a time for thinking, a time for playing and a time for dreaming.

Photo by: Gerald J. Schiffhorst

Writers need patience: If you wait, the words will come.

Photo by:
Gerald J. Schiffhorst

"A cat has absolute emotional honesty."

--Ernest Hemingway

"A home without a cat, and a well-fed, well-petted, and properly revered cat, may be a perfect home, *perhaps*, but how can it prove its title?"

--Mark Twain

"As an inspiration to the author, I do not think the cat can be over-estimated. . . . The perfect symmetry of his body urges one to achieve an equally perfect form. . . . Indeed the cat is as nearly as possible what many a writer would like to be himself."

--Carl Van Vechten

Part II. FROM VISIONS TO REVISIONS:
A PRACTICAL GUIDE TO WRITING

If you are a writer and want some practical advice on improving your writing skills, this part of the book will especially appeal to you. If you are not a writer, this part will interest you, too. Trust me.

As you know from Part I, cats are inspirational, but they are also serious, methodical, and persnickety. As such they can help us through the writing process, most obviously in the revising and polishing stage, when we lick a piece of prose into shape. The "writing process" is nothing new or mysterious;

it means simply the overlapping series of stages writers go through as they ponder, write, and re-write, sometimes simultaneously. You might think of the parts of the process as follows:

- Planning
- Drafting
- Revising
- Editing and proofreading.

You can't do all of these activities at one sitting, though some of my students try and feel frustrated as a result. If you have a cat, she can remind you to take things one at a time. She is incapable of grooming herself while also being attentive to the sounds of nature; the focus is on one <u>or</u> the other. Similarly, being mindful of the stages in the process of writing might also help you stay with one stage until you are ready for the next one.

AN OVERVIEW

What basic tools does a writer need? Most authors would say we learn most about writing by reading (absorbing the style of authors we admire) and by writing regularly, using the comments and suggestions of sensitive, experienced readers as we develop more skills in matching words to thoughts. An elaborate vocabulary and a perfect command of grammar are certainly not prerequisites. In fact, as Stephen King says in his memoir *On Writing*, if adults don't know the grammar of their native language through reading and conversation, there is little point in studying it. Still, he gives a few useful tips on usage and on fiction writing that you might enjoy. I have listed several other more comprehensive style guides in the Recommended Reading section.

My own development as a writer in college had nothing to do with writing courses or the study of grammar. Quite simply, I read voraciously and imitated the style of the authors I most admired; the comments of good teachers were encouraging and helpful, and I continue to learn new ways to improve a sentence. I keep a journal of memorable comments by writers and often use my various journal entries as seeds for my own work. My wife Lynn's first book of poetry, *Planting the Voice*, was based on her practice of "breaking off" a word or phrase from another poet's work and planting it, so to speak, in her own soil so that something new might take root. Many writers do something similar; they know that they are part of, and indebted to, a long literary tradition that is the source of their own inspiration. All writers imitate, someone said, and good writers often steal. Consider Shakespeare, who borrowed freely the stories for his plays. Of course, writers today give credit to their sources in an acknowledgement or footnote.

The main point is that good writers are, first of all, good readers who pay attention to the word choice and sentence patterns of what they read. I can't emphasize enough the importance of wide reading in the development of a writer's sense of structure, language, and tone.

But for many writers, no matter how much they have read, overcoming the fear of the blank page is a major problem: that is what this book is intended to address. As Stephen King says, "Good writing is often about letting go of fear and affectation." (And he knows a thing or two about fear.)

Trust yourself: know that the words that first come to mind as you think about your subject are probably the best, maybe the closest to representing your ideas. Don't strain for fancy phrases or worry about correctness. "Look in your heart and write," as Sir Philip Sidney said in one of his Elizabethan sonnets. If you don't have a strong feel for the material and an urge to communicate, your writing will go nowhere.

Finally, don't worry about being published or even read until you have finished your work:

enjoy the process of writing. In doing this book, I have had no idea whether anyone would like it well enough to read it. Just working on it has been a joy. Of course, I want readers, as every writer does; but I try to take the process one step at a time.

A Note on Fiction Writing

"There are three rules for writing a novel," the novelist Somerset Maugham wrote. "Unfortunately, nobody remembers what they are." Since I am not a fiction writer, I can't be much more helpful, but I hope most of the advice in this part of the book will apply to you in your writing of fiction. And I suggest a few sources to consult, such as the books by Stephen King and Jerome Stern in Recommended Reading. These authors, and teachers of creative writing, would probably agree that there are no "rules" for producing good fiction. The main things are to write and find sensitive readers to help you revise.

Mark Twain, in his comic essay "Fennimore Cooper's Literary Offenses" (1895) lists 18 "rules governing literary art in the domain of romantic fiction," including the following principles that have been ignored by many writers other than Cooper:

- "[T]he personages in a tale shall be alive, except in the case of corpses, and that always the reader shall be able to tell the corpses from the others. . . .
- [T]he personages in a tale, both dead and alive, shall exhibit a sufficient excuse for being there. . . .
- [W]hen the personages in a tale deal in conversation, the talk shall sound like human talk, and be talk such as human beings would be likely to talk in the given circumstances. . . .
- Use the right word, not its second cousin. . .
- Employ a simple and straightforward style."

Valuable advice.

BEING INVENTIVE

Getting started is often the hardest part of writing. Even if you are inspired by your cat, you might not know how to begin. Every writer works differently. Lynn, who writes for children, and I often get ideas from our reading and from talking with friends. We then jot down notes on any paper available, even napkins when we're in restaurants, then compose on the computer. It is important to begin with an overall plan or sense of purpose: why am I writing, and for whom? What is the main thing I want to express?

This doesn't mean you need a formal outline or always know where your story or article is going: if it's good, it will have a life of its own and will tell you where to take it.

The planning-thinking stage, also called invention, puts the focus on you and your purpose (more than on the reader) and might begin with a few basic questions:

- What do I know the most about?
- What I am most interested in sharing with readers?
- Am I you going to tell a story or explain something or argue a point? Maybe all three? Which will dominate?
- What main point(s) do I hope to make? Write these down.

You might invest in an inexpensive journal and keep notes there or put your separate slips of paper into the journal for safekeeping. The great thing about journal writing and notetaking is that, if you feel you are stuck for something to say, you have only to look at the sentences you have in front of you to realize that you have generated some material that you can use.

Composition teachers call this exploratory stage pre-writing, but, if you write out your brainstorming in sentences and phrases, whether in a rough outline or scribbled notes, **you are already writing**. If getting started was a problem, you have already broken through any negative barriers that can deter even experienced writers from beginning. If you write out a dozen sentences without stopping to see what you might say, chances are you will end up with a few points worth saving, and you will have answered some of those opening questions about your purpose in writing.

Remember that writing does not have to be done entirely at a desk, in front of a screen. Ideas will come in odd places. When I think of Lizzie in one of her sudden illuminations, she might be on the window sill or on top of the sofa. Your brainstorms might come in the shower, while taking a walk, or cooking a meal. No wonder writers have pencil and paper handy in most places (except the shower). Our house is littered with notes, drafts, and scraps of paper.

Inspiration might come at night, as it often does with me. Being nocturnal may be natural for cats, but it is not for most people. Many writers do their best work in the morning; what we read or think about in the evening percolates in the unconscious and, usually, when the mood is right, pours out for an hour or two the next morning. The 17th century poet John Milton, being blind, would ask one of his secretaries or daughters to read to him at night; he would then arise very early to begin dictating *Paradise Lost*, all 10,500 lines of it. He mentions that his muse visited his "slumbers nightly."

Julia Cameron, in *The Right to Write*, sensibly suggests writing any time you can fit it comfortably into your daily routine. Few writers have the luxury of concentrating full-time on their work.

Many writers say that they follow a strict regimen: four hours of writing every morning, followed by lunch, a nap, and exercise. Then they are ready for a return to work at night. Charles Dickens followed such a pattern. Another Victorian novelist, Anthony Trollope, worked for thirty-three years at the post office, but that did not stop him from writing more than fifty books: he trained himself to produce a certain number of words per hour each morning before going to work.   Stephen King says that he works every morning, every day of the year, aiming to produce 10 pages or about 2,000 words a day.

Not everyone is so disciplined—or prolific. Every writer must find his or her own schedule. If you are new to writing, I recommend writing something every day, perhaps a journal entry, so that writing becomes a habit.

Whatever time is best for you, I do <u>not</u> recommend the habit of many of my students, who postpone their essays as long as possible, then "pull an all-nighter." This is no fun, and the writing process should be enjoyed—savored even—not rushed. When I require a draft two weeks before the due date, many students are grateful because they have been forced to get a head start, and each time they return to their work, they will see it in a fresh way. This is the

ideal: draft or compose, re-write, then polish—
at different times, maybe on different days.
Each re-reading of our writing stimulates our
thinking and vocabulary.

Breaking up the writing process into stages is
essential. Few, if any, writers can think about
the content of a piece and its style at the same
time, giving equal attention to generating ideas,
organizing them, selecting words, shaping
sentences, not to mention polishing and editing.
Keep your focus on the <u>present</u> sentences you
are working on, and block out concerns about
what is ahead (or what you have or have not
done).

All of this is work and requires patience,
concentration, and courage in overcoming the
natural fears all writers face. If you feel
overwhelmed, keep your goal in mind: You are
writing every day because you care deeply about
what you have to say and want to share it with
others. Someone, eventually, will read and
appreciate your efforts. As Hemingway said,

"Writing must be a labor of love or it is not writing."

The idea that <u>writing is a process</u> means that good writing can rarely be done in one sitting. Allow yourself adequate time. Consider Lizzie or your own cat. Her day is neatly divided into discrete stages: mornings require a deliberate return to some activity, which usually involves grooming herself or hoping that I will stop and pet her. This is followed by quality porch time, where serious thinking and observation occur. After lunch, there is an extended nap, preferably in filtered sun. Note that all of these stages so far have been carefully planned. She knows what is best for her and gives careful consideration to finding just what she needs—even if on a freshly made bed.

My wife, Lynn, and I try to imitate her afternoon siesta ritual whenever we can but are ready for bed around 11 p.m., when Lizzie is in top form, racing from room to room, chasing her favorite catnip-flavored mouse or one of my shoelaces and, at times, having one of her sudden bursts of illumination: she will stop suddenly and stare straight ahead. If only I could write down what she is thinking at such moments!

I would like to think that Lizzie's frantic nocturnal activity is a cover for what writers call invention; if she were a writer, she could be looking for ideas and for ways to say them effectively. She has created for herself a world of pure imagination and is not deterred by our eagerness to sleep.

Perhaps the main lesson we learn from Lizzie's daily routine is not to spend too much time at any one thing. Being eminently practical, cats like Lizzie know instinctively to rest in preparation for every round of activity; and so she lives in an ideal equilibrium between action and contemplation. She is serious yet also playful and is much too sensible ever to overdo anything. Even the sublime catnip is something to return to. There is a time for resting and a time for thinking, a time for playing and a time for dreaming. Is there a lesson here for us—whether we are writers or not?

By the way, in her book, *The Tribe of Tiger*, the science writer Elizabeth Marshall Thomas suggests that cats sometimes try to teach us things: in bringing prey for us to admire, they perhaps want us to learn how to hunt. So my idea that a cat can be a writer's best teacher might have a biological basis after all. Lizzie certainly thinks through her options before deciding where to go in the house: she has a basic plan in mind, something writers, too, must have. The parts will fit together logically if you begin with a sense of where you are going.

Here are a few other basic principles for the first stage in writing:

- Space your work out over as many days as possible; with each re-reading of your text, you will see new things.

- Take plenty of time to think and take notes. Such time is never wasted. Lizzie is not the only one in our family who spends quality time gazing out the window.

- Take time to play and stretch.

- Don't force writing: like cats, we are not always in the mood.

- Read the work of your favorite published writers and soak up their style.

- Be patient with yourself. Do not force yourself to conform to artificial deadlines. And never rush.

- If you are enthusiastic about your topic, and aware of your experience as a reader, the chances are excellent that you will produce good, readable prose. Never hesitate to give yourself positive reinforcement. We all need affirmations, especially writers working alone.

- Take time assembling ideas and observations so that you have plenty of material to drawn from. Take notes on what you see. Lizzie misses nothing in her observations; careful writers can follow her example.

- Follow a plan or outline, but do not hesitate to change it as new ideas develop, as they will.

- Write about what you know best; even so, some research is often needed. To develop a piece successfully, you need colorful details, facts, and examples.

- Take care of editing later; do not worry about style or correctness until you have finished your drafting. Keep yourself in present time.

BUILDING CONFIDENCE

You've heard of "writer's block." Perhaps you have experienced it: staring at a blank screen or paper for hours, wondering what to say (and worrying that no one will care after you have said it). You might even find yourself agreeing with the observation of Thomas Mann: "A writer is somebody for whom writing is more difficult than it is for other people." Perhaps he meant that real writers have to revise, revise, and revise again. I hope that you won't be discouraged, even momentarily, by this and that my overview of the writing process will help you develop greater confidence in yourself as a writer (and future author).

What is often not widely discussed is something I call "English block": many people say, "if I were a writer, I could tell quite a story; but English was never my strong suit." They are defeated before they begin.

What this reveals is a mistaken notion that writing is an art bestowed on only a talented few, rather than a craft that can be learned and worked at. Your work in English class years ago may have been mediocre, your command of grammar faulty, your lack of expertise in editing apparent—but none of these things should deter you. If you can speak the English language, why can't you write it? If you really want to write, you can! I know many writers, including some academic colleagues, who worry about "grammar rules," which have nothing to do with the main stages of writing. By this I mean that drafting and even revising are quite separate from editing (correcting the errors we all make). Premature editing—and a fear of being criticized, of re-living an English-class embarrassment---has done more to cripple would-be writers than anything I know. We learn to write by writing—and by reading good authors, not by studying books of grammar. If a strong command of grammar and usage were essential to success as a writer, how many bestsellers in the last fifty years would have been written? Very few!

In dealing with English block, you might ask, What Would My Cat Do? Lizzie, like all cats, is incapable of worrying about what might happen and, living fully in the present, reminds me to take one step at a time. In hunting a lizard on the porch, does she stop to think she might not catch it or that she is not as skillful as other cats or that some more experienced cat would come by and criticize her? Of course not. So why should I worry about editing what I write until I have finished writing it? I cannot worry about who is going to read an article, much less publish it, until I find out what I have to say. Stay in the first stage of the writing process.

One great aspect of this process is that what you do in the early stages can help you build confidence: you come to realize that **You Know Much More Than You Think You Know**. I highlight this maxim because students over the years who have heard me say it have invariably been helped in overcoming their fears of being inadequate. Writers often forget how much they have read and experienced in their lives and how this wealth of insight can easily be tapped into— if they think of themselves and their work affirmatively, not critically or fearfully. A fundamental rule in writing is to write about what you know.

Don't tell yourself that you are really not much of an expert on gardening or travel or basketball or that there are hundreds of books and articles on such subjects you have never read. Instead, trust yourself that you already know quite a bit and are highly motivated to learn more and share your insights with others. If you were not highly motivated, would you be a writer at all? If you allow what you don't know to dominate your thinking, your creative composing will never get off the ground.

One of the challenges of writing is that it requires a certain amount of isolation. Like cats, writers spend time quietly, alone, thinking, observing, composing, and revising. For many busy people, this time spent in solitude is a blessing. The full-time writer, however, who forgets to break up his or her workday into manageable segments can come to dread time spent alone.

But I wonder if we are really alone. If we think of ourselves "talking" to our imagined readers and being interconnected with others writing on similar subjects, we find ourselves in what Thomas Merton called a "friendly communion of silence." He was referring to contemplative prayer. As both monk and writer, Merton sought greater and greater solitude yet never really felt isolated but spiritually related to countless unseen people.

If you don't want to consider Merton, consider your cat--your silent, spiritual partner who replicates the cats that aided the great writers mentioned in part I. Even if Lizzie and all the other cats awake at this moment are not part of some "feline internet," silently communicating with one another, as Lynn once suggested, we know that Lizzie is connected to us.

When I hear myself talking to her in a language that she cannot fully understand, I know that I am not alone: everyone talks to their pets. Cats, I find, are very good listeners. They never interrupt or contradict what we say. And it might help in the brainstorming part of writing, especially, to "talk things out" with your cat. Read your first draft aloud—even your initial ideas—to see how they sound. Hearing yourself say what you plan to commit to paper is helpful. If it feels awkward to talk to yourself, address yourself to your cat. She who inspired you should be your first audience.

REVISION: LICKING WRITING INTO SHAPE

Most revision or re-writing occurs after you have completed a draft and feel satisfied that you have included most of your "visions" or ideas; you feel that you now have something to say. Whereas your planning and drafting focused mainly on you—your ideas and their development—revision puts more emphasis on the reader. It is not easy to see your work from the reader's point of view, but it is important to read your drafts (yes, there will be many) as if you were an objective outsider. Begin by considering carefully who your readers are, what they need to be told, what they already know, and what they need to be satisfied.

CONSIDERING THE READER

Advice on writing always includes suggestions about keeping the reader in mind as you work. In *Writing with Style*, John R. Trimble gives these two valuable tips for writing readable prose:

> Write with the assumption that your reader is a companionable friend with a warm sense of humor and an appreciation of simple straightforwardness.
> Write as if you were actually talking to that friend, but talking with enough leisure to frame your thoughts concisely and interestingly. (77)

If you like this advice as much as I do, you might post Trimble's tips over your desk.

Capturing the reader's interest usually involves spending a lot of creative energy on your introduction. After all, it is the first thing, along with the title, that the reader sees, and it must be inviting. Notice how many journalists begin with an imaginative example or case study before stating their main idea. Other writers open with questions. I began a recent essay with the question, "Do you think your life is important—in the big scheme of things?" I wanted to stop the reader, force him or her to think--and to read on. Many writers use quotations, sometimes amusing ones, but you have to be careful that your humor is appropriate for the purpose and tone of your piece. If you want to surprise the reader, you might use a quotation, an unusual fact or example so that your introduction is lively. I generally advise students to return to their opening paragraphs after their revision is complete and put extra time on making the opening interesting. Without a strong introduction that tells readers why they should continue to read, your purpose in writing will fall flat.

"Creativity is continual surprise," the science-fiction writer Ray Bradbury said.

Writers must keep their readers in a state of "near perpetual surprise," Trimble advises. "Not suspense, but surprise. It's like baseball. A skilled pitcher mixes up his pitches. He'll throw a fast ball, then a curve....Skilled writers work much the same way. They're constantly feeding the reader's appetite for novelty, be it with a fresh idea, a fresh phrase, or a fresh image." (65)

Revision takes time. It means "looking again"; it means to rethink and clarify what you have written so that it is clear to someone else. You step back from your work and examine it with fresh eyes. As Donald M. Murray, a distinguished writing teacher, has said, "there is no writing without re-writing." Every writer goes through this often lengthy process. Ernest Hemingway revised the ending of *A Farewell to Arms* 39 times; when asked later what problem he was having, he said, "Getting the words right." Your work probably won't need 39 revisions, but it is important to remember that revision is quite separate from editing (making corrections).

Some Tips:

- Discard anything from your draft that does not relate to your main point.
- Read your work aloud: if a sentence sounds awkward, rework it until it sounds right.
- Let someone else (preferably someone who reads a lot) read over your draft and react honestly to a few questions, such as: Does it make sense?
  Am I making essentially one point? Do I provide enough examples or descriptive details?
- Revise in stages; each time you return to it, you will see it in a new light. The stages Donald Murray recommends are three: Revise for overall meaning, revise for organization, and revise for style. I will comment on each of these.

<u>Revise for overall meaning</u>. Read your draft quickly, looking only at the following questions:

- What is my main point or controlling idea? What am I trying to say, in a sentence? Teachers often call this a thesis statement, and it is essential to having your work hang together and say one thing—even if you don't have an explicit thesis.

- Is this main point clearly stated somewhere in the opening? It is good practice to specify your main idea, the way journalists usually do. But many writers—including fiction writers—do not follow this practice.

- Does everything I say relate to that main point? Check each paragraph to see if it supports your major idea, and delete irrelevant points, no matter how interesting they may seem.

- Do I have enough evidence/examples/details to develop my point? This is perhaps the greatest challenge for the beginning writer. Many of my students rely on generalizations without supporting them with examples; as a result, their work is not convincing.

- Is the draft too short? If so, what more should I add? If you have an assigned word length, it is easy to see if your first draft is close to the minimum. Looking at your notes should provide you with more material.

- If the draft is too long, what can be cut? Most good drafts end up being fuller than they need to be. You have put into the draft nearly everything you have discovered from reading and thinking about the topic. Painful though it may be to delete some of your sentences or paragraphs, remember your audience: too many examples of the same type can be redundant and boring.

2. <u>Revise for organization</u>. Read the draft again, with these things in mind:

- Do I have a good title and introduction that will capture the reader's interest? Remember that this is the first thing the reader will see and should be sufficiently original and eye-catching to make him or her want to read on. Your job as a writer is to keep the reader's attention. Working over and over the introduction often takes more of my time than revising other parts of an essay or article.

- Is every paragraph related to my main idea? We're back again to unity: am I saying essentially one thing? Is anything extraneous? If so, cut it.

- Are my paragraphs developed with adequate facts and examples? If the paragraph looks skimpy, chances are it needs more development.

- Am I bringing myself into the piece too much? An autobiographical or personal essay can be expected to focus on you as observer and narrator, and basic to any writing is to write about what we know. But if you find that nearly every sentence in your draft of an informative piece includes the first person {"I"), you are not putting proper focus on your subject. As you describe a travel experience, for example, does the reader want to know how you felt as you looked at a mountain, or do you want to show the reader the mountain? Students are often taught in high school to avoid the first person entirely so that the focus of their writing is not on themselves. (Some of my students go to extremes, fearing to use the first person in any college writing.)

- Is there a conclusion that sums up my main points? Endings can be tricky since you don't want to be too obvious and simply restate your main points; still, you want the reader to make a connection between your opening and your conclusion and feel satisfied that what you promised in the introduction has been fulfilled. My general advice: be brief in restating your main idea and never introduce new material in the conclusion.

3. <u>Revise for Style.</u> After a break, return to your draft, reading it aloud, slowly, and paying attention to the following questions:

- Are all the sentences starting the same way (subject, verb, object)? Could I use subordination (when, because, although, etc.) to add variety?

- Are any sentences overloaded? If so, break them in half so the reader does not get confused.

- Are my sentences varied in length (not all too short or too long)?

- Are my sentences parallel in structure: nouns with nouns, verbs with verbs, etc., as in *to write, to revise, and to edit?*

- Am I using concrete, specific nouns and vivid verbs, rather than relying on adjectives and adverbs such as *very, beautifully,* etc.

- Do I lead the reader smoothly from one point to the next, using transitions (*moreover, however,* etc.)

- Am I repeating myself or using trite, wordy expressions?

- Are my tenses (past, present, future) consistent

- Is my point of view (person: *I, you, they,* etc.) consistent?

- Are there any words whose meanings I am unsure of?

There are other stylistic issues to consider. Consult a handbook on composition, which will also include many more grammatical elements than I list below, or one of the books I include under Recommended Reading.

But it is easy to be overwhelmed by the revision stage. Each time you return to your work you can look for something else. But when you wonder if all the work is worthwhile, you can remember this remark by Mark Twain and laugh: "Writing is easy; all you have to do is cross out the wrong words."

<u>Any</u> piece of writing can be improved by stylistic revision, especially by reducing wordiness. Cicero reportedly wrote to a friend: "I would have written you a shorter letter if I had had more time." It takes time to revise.

Notice how your cat takes her time with her daily toilette. Lizzie devotes half an hour each day to her tail alone, for reasons known only to her. That is why I call this section "licking" your prose into shape because it is the part of writing most obviously analogous to what cats do daily; they give this activity the same focused attention as the other aspects of their lives. For me, rewriting has always been my favorite part of writing, and word processing has made all aspects of revision enjoyable. I particularly enjoy seeing how I can shorten what I have written. George Orwell, author of *1984* and other books, has an influential essay on the abuses of the English language, at the end of which he makes these stylistic recommendations about finding fresh ways of stating things:

i. Never use a metaphor, simile, or other figure of speech which you are used to seeing in print.

ii. Never use a long word where a short one will do.

iii.   If it is possible to cut out a word, always cut it out.

iv.   Never use the passive [e.g., it was reported] when you can use the active [he reported]

v.   Never use a foreign phrase, a scientific word or a jargon word if you can think of an everyday English equivalent.

vi.   Break any of these rules sooner than say anything outright barbarous.

("Politics and the English Language," *A Collection of Essays by George Orwell* (Garden City: Doubleday, 1954), p. 176.

Orwell's first principle involves clichés. Like every other book on writing, my *Short Handbook for Writers* has a section on avoiding trite expressions as much as possible and advises writers to look for original ways of saying things. Many fresh metaphors have long gone stale.

Some examples: *nipped in the bud, bottom line, can of worms.* Since you (I hope) have a feline literary partner, be especially mindful of the following odious expressions, many of them going back to the days when cats were often hated, abused, or merely tolerated:

- There's more than one way to skin a cat.
- It looked like something the cat dragged in.
- Has the cat got your tongue?
- Don't let the cat out of the bag.

A little guidebook on usage and style that has helped several generations of American writers is *The Elements of Style* by Strunk and White, which I highly recommend. Please see Recommended Reading for some other suggestions.

NEVER SAY 'NEVER'

If you had one of those English teachers who insisted that you never do x or y and you still worry about making mistakes before you have a chance to make any, keep in mind that there are exceptions to nearly all grammar rules. After all, these rules are not divine commands or scientific laws but, like everything in language, subject to change. Here are a few outdated prohibitions:

1. Never start a sentence with *there*. This advice is well-intentioned but too sweeping: sometimes, you must open a sentence with *there*. Teachers are concerned that there is a weak beginning because it delays the real subject of the sentence: "There are many writers who have loved cats." (The real subject here is *writers*, so put this first: Many writers have loved cats.) Still, there are times (as in this sentence) when *there* belongs there.

2. Never split infinitives. An infinitive is the basic form of the verb, expressed with to, as in "to sleep, perchance to dream." Victorian-era grammarians began to frown on inserting words (to *gently* sleep) that split the infinitive,

basing their rules on Latin grammar. This is a useless taboo that writers have long ignored or been unaware of.

3. Never end a sentence with a preposition. Another ridiculous taboo, based on Latin grammar rather than English usage. Prepositions such as *on, off, in, with, to,* might sound awkward at the end of a sentence, but so does Winston Churchill's famous send-up: "Ending a sentence with a preposition is something up with which I will not put." In her amusing and helpful guide to grammar, *Woe Is I,* Patricia O'Conner uses three prepositions at the end of a sentence about a "rule that modern grammarians have long tried to get us out from under."

4. Never start a sentence with and or but. But writers often do, with good reason (as I just did). And yet my students continue to ask if it's permissible (now that they're older) to use *and* or *but* to open sentences. Yes!

5. Never use *who* when you need *whom*. In informal writing, as in conversation, *who* is acceptable, even though *whom* might be more formally correct: "To whom is the note addressed?" This is very stiff compared with, "Who's the note addressed to?" O'Conner wisely recommends reversing the order of a question such as the formally correct "From whom?" to "Who from?"

A related issue is the misuse of "I/me," based on old fears of using the wrong form, so when in doubt many people opt for *I*, even when me is grammatical: "Lizzie brought the lizard to Lynn and I." Would you say she brought the lizard "to I"? Of course not. Use *I* for the subject position (Lynn and I are writers), use *me* for the object position ("me" is the object of to). And it is technically correct to say, "It is I," "That is he," etc., but there is nothing wrong with using "It's me" or "That's him," especially if you want your writing to sound natural, like spoken English.

6. Never use the passive voice. Good writers generally avoid the passive, which can be

awkward and wordy: "The ball was chased by Lizzie." Would anyone talk this way? The active voice is better because it is closer to the way we speak; the subject does something: "Lizzie chased the ball." This is more direct, natural, and concise than putting the object (*ball*) first. Bureaucrats often hide behind the passive voice: "The report will be issued tomorrow." Who will issue it? (Note: the passive has nothing to do with past tense.) But there are legitimate uses for the passive, when emphasizing the doer is inappropriate or unnecessary: "George W. Bush was elected president in 2000." Or "Jake's article will be published next month."

EDITING: BEING *PURR*TICULAR and *PURR*SNICKETY

The final part of the revision process is for many writers the most tedious since it requires them to remember dozens of rules they never fully learned. Many authors rely on professional editors to help them, but you can be your own editor. You don't need special courses in grammar to do the job. The main thing to recall is that errors will distract the reader from the effectiveness of what you are trying to communicate and make you look less authoritative as a writer. A good writer is as fussy as a cat picking off fleas and polishing her fur. Lizzie, like all cats, has very high standards and has inspired this little list of nine PET PEEVES. They only account for a few of the distracting errors that bother good readers, but they are among the most common:

Please don't use **'s** for plurals (when you have
  more than one thing):
    NOT: three kitten's.
    BUT: three kittens. To form a plural, just
    add **s** to most words. Lynn, Lizzie, and I
    are the Schiffhorsts, not the
    Schiffhorst's. Just add **s** for the plural.

By the way, there is a difference between **'s**
and **s'**: our kitten's toy (for one kitten). For
more than one: Our kittens' toys are at the

Schiffhorsts' house. [or at the Schiffhorst residence]

It's means <u>only one thing</u>: it is. There are few absolutes in grammar, but this is one—a term often misused. If you want to say it's raining, use the apostrophe to indicate a contraction--that the *is* has been shortened. Otherwise, use *its* (as in *his, hers, theirs, ours*): The tree has lost some of its leaves.

Use the semicolon (;) between complete clauses rather than run them together:

> NOT: The new vet could see that Lizzie was healthy, he only gave her a routine examination.
> BUT: The new vet could see that Lizzie was healthy; he only gave her a routine examination. (OR , so he only gave her... OR Because the new vet...)

Check your subjects to make sure you are being logical and polite:

NOT: Me and Lizzie are home alone
tonight. [Only small children are allowed
to put themselves first.]
BUT: Lizzie and I are home alone tonight.

Some people worry so much about misusing
certain words that they forget the basics:

NOT: Lizzie presented her dead lizard to
Lynn and I. (to I?)
BUT: Lizzie presented her dead lizard to
Lynn and me. (to me)

Make sure that your verbs agree with their
subjects:

NOT: Tuna *taste* great to most cats.
BUT: Tuna *tastes* great to most cats.

7. Some writers use too many unnecessary
words:

Use *in fact*, not *in point of fact*
Use *because*, not *due to the fact that*

8. Make sure you have the right word:

> NOT: The neighbors' cat is *laying* in our yard.

> BUT: The neighbors' cat is *lying* in our yard.

Avoid unintentionally sexist language:

> NOT: Every writer has his own story to tell.

> NOT: Every writer has their own story to tell.

> BUT: Every writer has his or her own story to tell

> OR EVEN BETTER: Writers have their own stories to tell. (Avoid the problem by making the subject plural.)

Finally, do you have the right tools for editing? I mean a sharp pencil, a good dictionary, a thesaurus, and a handbook of grammar and usage.

PROOFREADING

As William Safire, *The New York Times* columnist has written, "You may think your eyes are sharp, but nothing beats a different pair of eyes." True, but writers usually must do their own initial proofing. One tip: print your draft, then starting with the last sentence and moving forwards, read each line with pencil in hand so that you don't focus on the content. Do this after you have put your final draft aside for a while. Usually when we read, our eyes move across a line of print in a series of "jumps" that allow us to focus on one point of information at a time. In proofreading, we must interrupt this usual method of reading and look at the words as words, checking the spelling, the grammar, and mechanics, not focusing on the meaning. In a famous 1631 edition of the King James Bible, the printer omitted a crucial not in the list of the Ten Commandments: "Thou shalt commit adultery." In the centuries since, most publications have included a "corrections" page to list bloopers that careful editors missed.

I hope that the above Pet Peeves will help you remind you of your own need to be "purrticular."

A FINAL WORD

Receiving and benefiting from positive criticism is important for every writer, irrespective of his or her experience. This is why many people take courses in writing or join writers' groups so that they can get honest feedback from careful readers about whether a draft flows coherently, is sufficiently interesting and well-developed to hold the reader's interest. Fellow writers can also be good sources of publication possibilities. Of course, you have to find helpful readers whom you trust.

If you ever find yourself feeling discouraged about getting published, remember the struggle that celebrated writers have gone through—and the discouraging reviews that famous works have received. Consider the following negative assessments of a few classics:

- "M. Flaubert is not a writer." From a review of *Madame Bovary* (1857)

- "*The Great Gatsby* is an absurd story, whether considered as a romance, melodrama, or plain record of New York high life." From a 1925 review of F. Scott Fitzgerald's classic novel.

- "The book is an emotional hodgepodge; no mood is sustained long enough to register for more than a chapter." From a *New York Times* review of Joseph Heller's *Catch-22* (1961).

To read more enlightening criticism of this type, see the little book, *Rotten Reviews*, edited by Bill Henderson (Penguin).

Nearly every published writer has had more rejections than acceptances, along with much criticism; all of this is part of the learning process. Writers continually learn by doing and by seeing how editorial comments and suggestions are essential to making their texts more readable. By risking their words and ideas before a critical public, they grow stronger in the ongoing struggle to express clearly what often seems impossible to find words for. "Getting the words right" was Hemingway's problem in 1929 and is every writer's challenge. I wish you the best in meeting this challenge, and I hope that all the feline virtues, especially patience, will inspire you in whatever you write.

RECOMMENDED READING

A. WRITING

Cameron, Julia. *The Right to Write.* New York: Putnam, 1998.

Keyes, Ralph. *The Courage to Write.* New York: Holt, 1995.

King, Stephen. *On Writing.* New York: Scribner, 2000.

Murray, Donald M. *The Craft of Revision.* New York: Dryden Press, 2000.

O'Conner, Patricia T. *Woe is I: The Grammarphobe's Guide to Better English in Plain English.* New York: Riverhead, 1996.

Schiffhorst, Gerald J. and Donald Pharr. *The Short Handbook for Writers*, 2nd ed. New York: McGraw-Hill, 1997.

Stern, Jerome. *Making Shapely Fiction.* New York: Norton, 1991.

Strunk, William and E. B. White. *The Elements of Style*, 3rd ed. New York: Macmillan, 1979.

Zinsser, William. *On Writing Well: The Classic Guide to Writing Non-Fiction.* New York: Harper, 2001.

B. CATS AND INSPIRATION

Amory, Cleveland. *The Cat Who Came for Christmas.* New York: Penguin, 1988.

Burden, Jean. *A Celebration of Cats.* New York: Eriksson, 1974.

Caras, Roger A. *A Cat is Watching.* New York: Simon & Schuster, 1989.

Carse, James P. "A Philosopher Needs a Cat." *Breakfast at the Victory: The Mysticism of Ordinary Experience.* San Francisco: Harper, 2000. Pp.19-31.

Lessing, Doris. *Particularly Cats.* New York: Knopf, 1991.

Lockridge, Francis and Richard. *Cats and People.* New York: Kodansha, 1996.

Loxton, Howard. *99 Lives: Cats in History, Legend and Literature.* London: Duncan Baird, 1998.

Masson, Jeffrey M. *The Nine Emotional Lives of Cats.* New York: Ballantine, 2002.

Méry, Fernand. *The Life, History and Magic of the Cat*, trans. Emma Street. New York: Grosset & Dunlap, 1968.

Oates, Joyce Carol and Daniel Halpern, eds. *The Sophisticated Cat.* New York: Dutton, 1992.

Piercy, Marge. *Sleeping with Cats.* New York: Morrow, 2001.

Rogers, Katherine M. *The Cat and the Human Imagination.* Ann Arbor: U of Michigan Press, 1998.

Sarton, May. *The Fur Person.* New York: Norton, 1983.

Thomas, Elizabeth Marshall. *The Tribe of Tiger.* New York: Simon & Schuster, 1994.

PART III. YOUR JOURNAL: WRITING WITH CATS

The pages in this section are intended to encourage you to make some notes about the writing process. Even if you are in the habit of keeping a journal, the blank spaces here might be a welcome invitation to react to what I have suggested about the relation between cats and writers.

Most writers keep a journal, just as most artists keep sketchbooks, to record impressions that they can later develop. Journal entries can be in the form of phrases, words, sentences, whole paragraphs, quotations, sayings— anything that occurs to you in your observations and that will prompt you to write when you read over your jottings. Think of a journal as a handy place to keep notes—and as a way to get started. If you think you have nothing to say, you can easily disprove this by seeing how much material you generate in your journal with a few prompts. That is why I include questions at the top of each page in this section--to get you started. No doubt many other questions will come to mind.

Have fun!

1. Cats have natural prey, and writers naturally turn toward topics they feel most attracted to. What <u>subjects</u> appeal most to you? Write these down. Remember the maxim: write about what you know best.

2. Cats, as we have seen, are <u>observant</u>. How can this help you? What things do you observe around you today that might be worth recording?

3. Cats put themselves first and never let themselves go. How much <u>priority attention</u> do you think your writing deserves? How many hours a day can you set aside to write?

4. Cats follow a "schedule" of sorts, with a daily pattern of napping, grooming, and playing. What <u>time of the day</u> works best for you? Morning? Night? Can you set aside an hour or two each day for writing, or does this seem too rigid?

5. What do you mean by <u>meditation and contemplation</u>? Perhaps the cat's daily reveries will give you an idea. How does this often wordless activity relate to writing? Can you make sure that meditation time is not seen as wasted?

6. Cats are comfortable <u>being alone</u> much of the time. What about you? Can you work comfortably alone for more than an hour? Is it better for you to write for shorter periods several times a day?

7. Cats give grooming the same focused attention as everything else. Writers have to <u>re-write</u> and edit their own work. Does this bother you? What is your experience with revision? What works for you?

8. Cats are neat and orderly. Writers, too, have to follow some clear, <u>orderly plan</u> so that their work is organized. What works best for you—an outline, a list, a series of notes that you later number?

9. Cats live in the present. But writers often worry about what lies ahead, especially the <u>conventions</u> of punctuation, grammar, and spelling. What is the best way for you to deal with these editing issues? Can you put them off entirely until your work is finished?

10. If you find yourself rushing through the writing process, remember the stately pace of cats, who take their time with each separate activity. Do you find it hard to <u>slow down</u> and separate the early stages of writing from the later stages of re-writing?

11. Describe briefly your <u>experience with writing</u>, whether in school, on the job, or whatever. What did you most like about it? What was the greatest challenge? How does thinking about the overall writing process, with its various steps, help you?

12. What role has <u>reading</u> played in your development as a writer? List a few of your favorite authors, those whose style you most admire. What skills can you learn by re-reading their work before you write? Or do you think that reading these authors would inhibit your own writing?

ABOUT THE AUTHOR

Gerald J. Schiffhorst, Professor Emeritus of English at the University of Central Florida, has taught writing and literature courses for more than 35 years. He has published eight books, including several editions of McGraw-Hill's *Short Handbook for Writers,* and numerous articles and reviews in national and international journals on literature and spirituality.

A native of St. Louis, Schiffhorst was educated at St. Louis University, the University of Illinois, and Washington University-St. Louis, where he received his Ph.D. He currently serves on the board of *Florida English* and is a speaker and editorial consultant.

He lives with his wife, Lynn, and their cat, Lizzie, in Winter Park, Florida.

See his website: **www.writingcats.com**. Or contact him at **schiffhorst@yahoo.com**.